Colour Ocean: Tropical Paradise

Adult Colouring for Relaxation

by J. Benson

Copyright © 2015 J. Benson et al

All rights reserved.

ISBN-10: 1519374623
ISBN-13: 978-1519374622

Adult Colouring for Relaxation

Colour Ocean: Tropical Paradise is an adult colouring book containing over forty pages of beautiful oceanic patterns designed specifically to help achieve a state of relaxation. Colour them in with a pen or pencil to help find your own state of inner peace and tranquility.

Colour Ocean: Tropical Paradise

Adult Colouring for Relaxation

by J. Benson

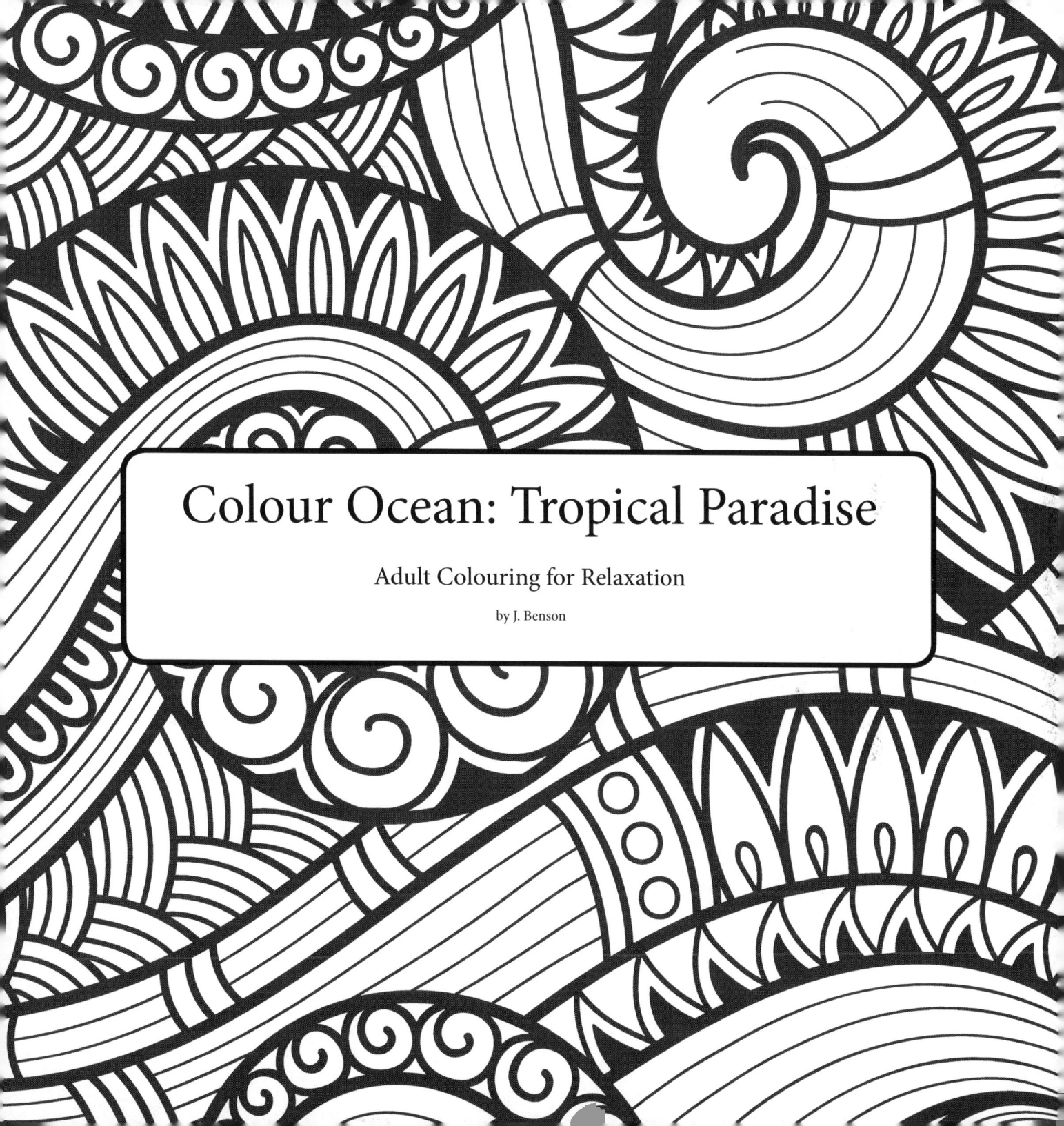

Colour Ocean: Tropical Paradise

Adult Colouring for Relaxation

by J. Benson

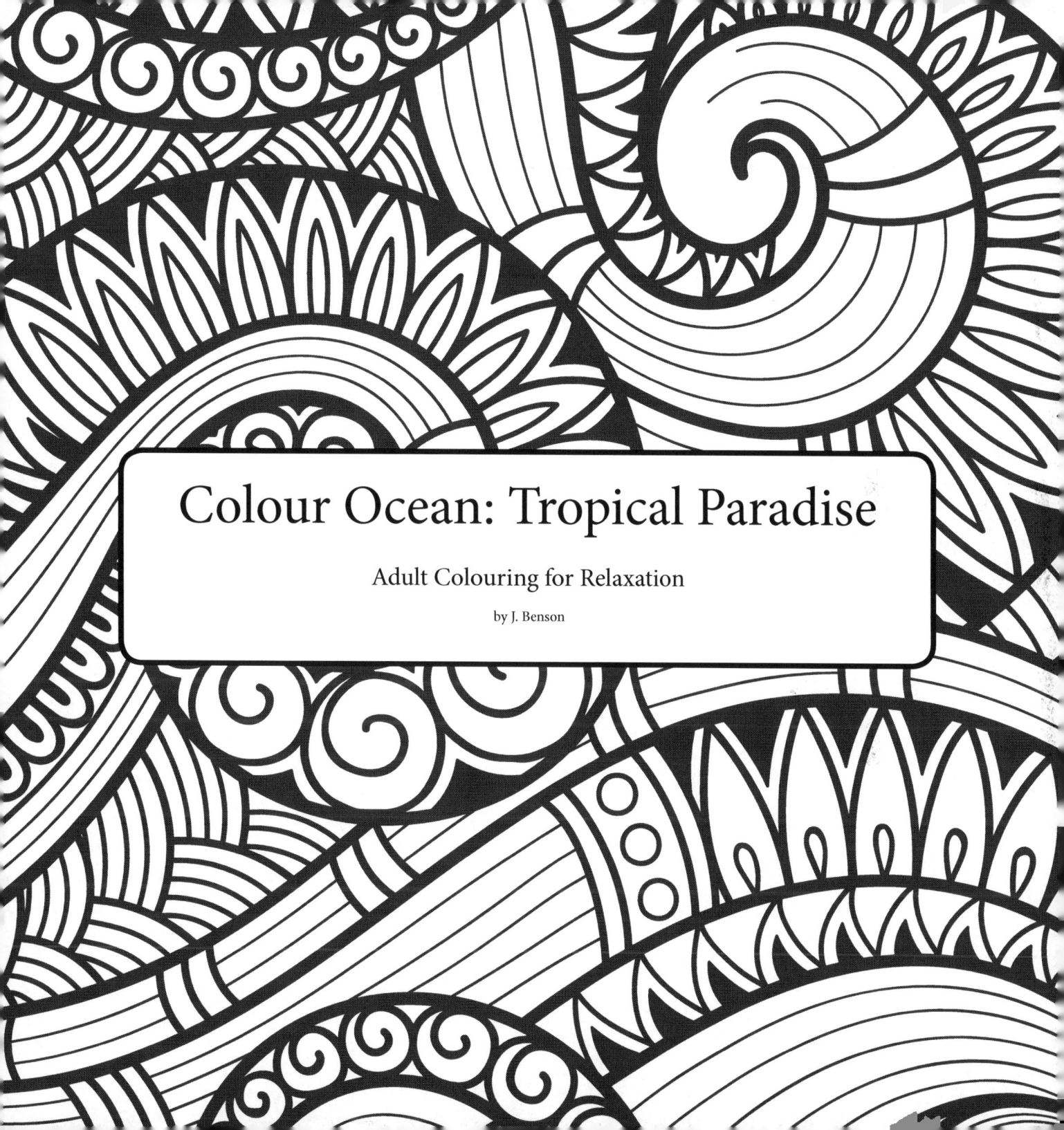

Colour Ocean: Tropical Paradise

Adult Colouring for Relaxation

by J. Benson

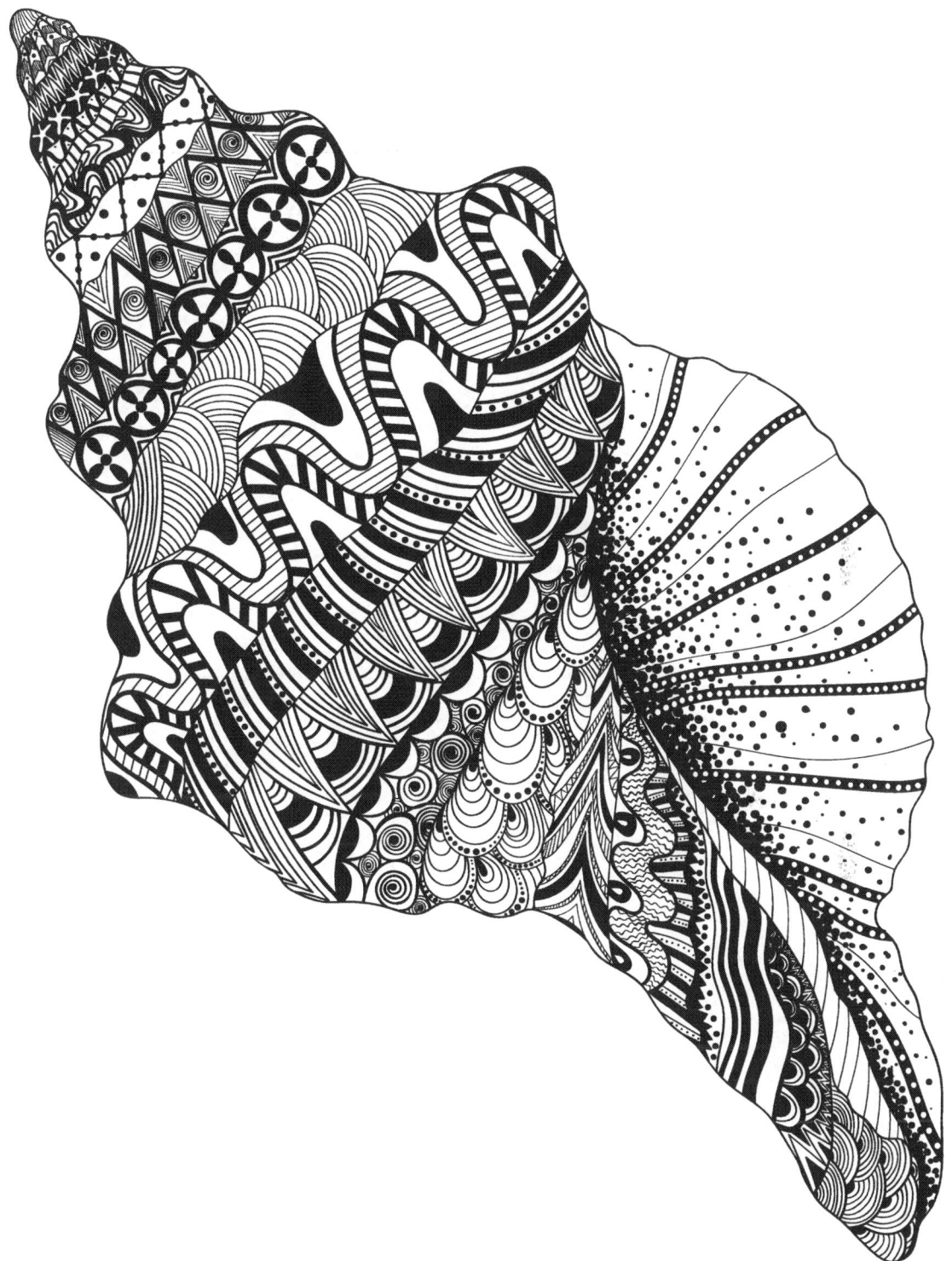

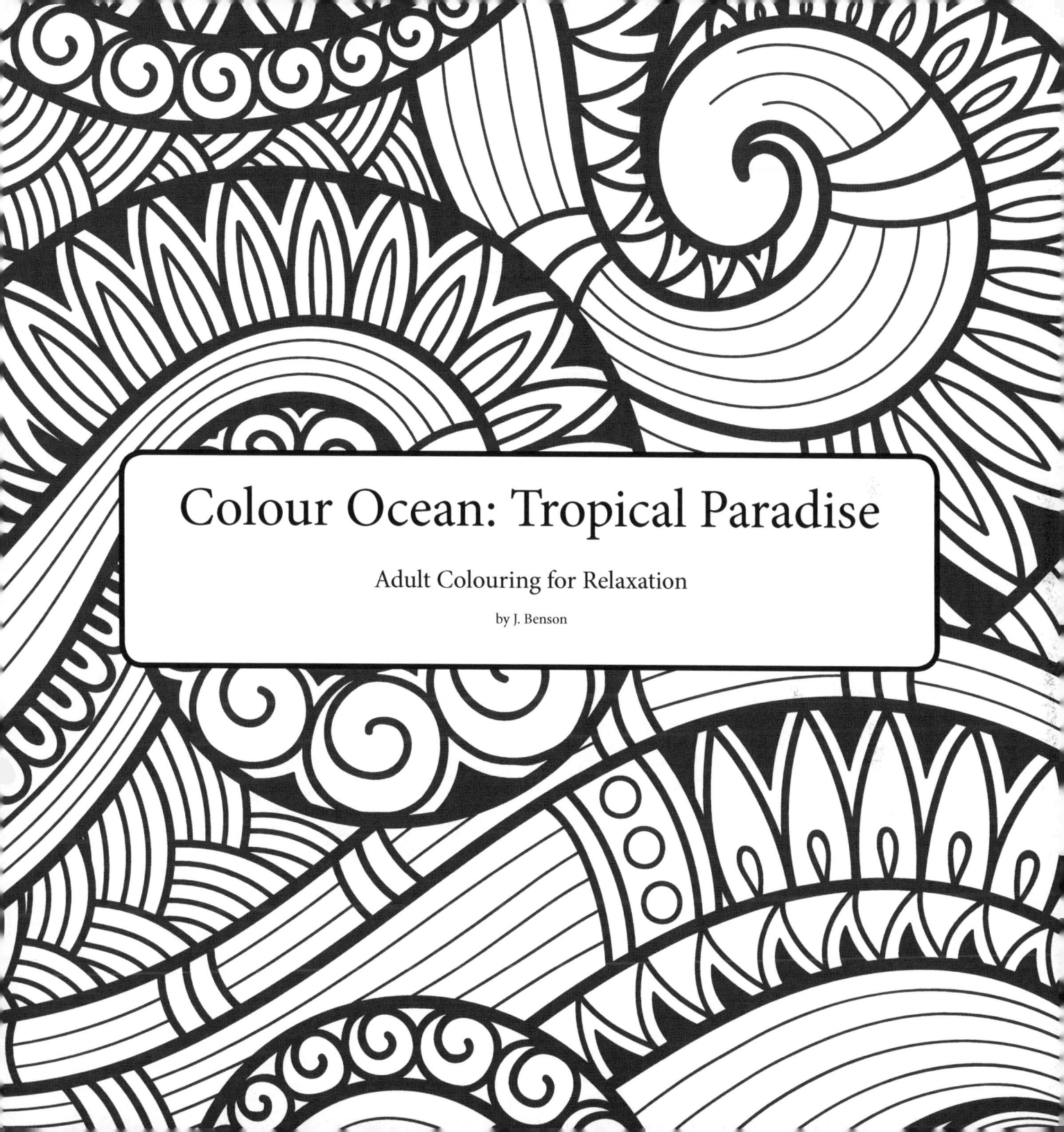

Colour Ocean: Tropical Paradise

Adult Colouring for Relaxation

by J. Benson

Interlude

You have a voice

Are you enjoying your experience? The world wants to hear your voice! Whether you love or loath this book, your feedback can make all the difference when someone is deciding whether it's right for them! When you have the opportunity, please visit Amazon or your favourite social network and share your thoughts by leaving a review or rating of this book.

Thank you,

Jack

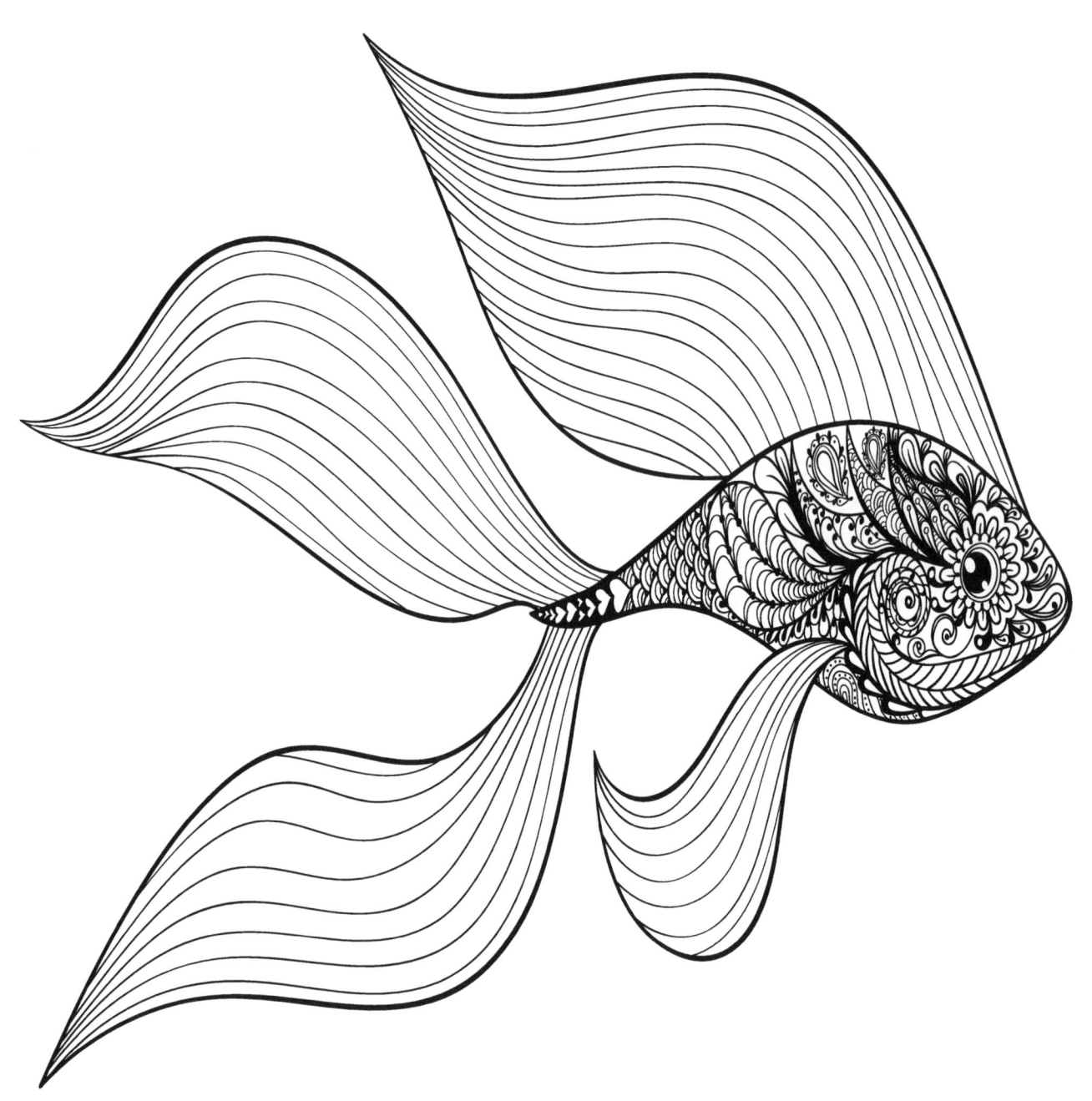

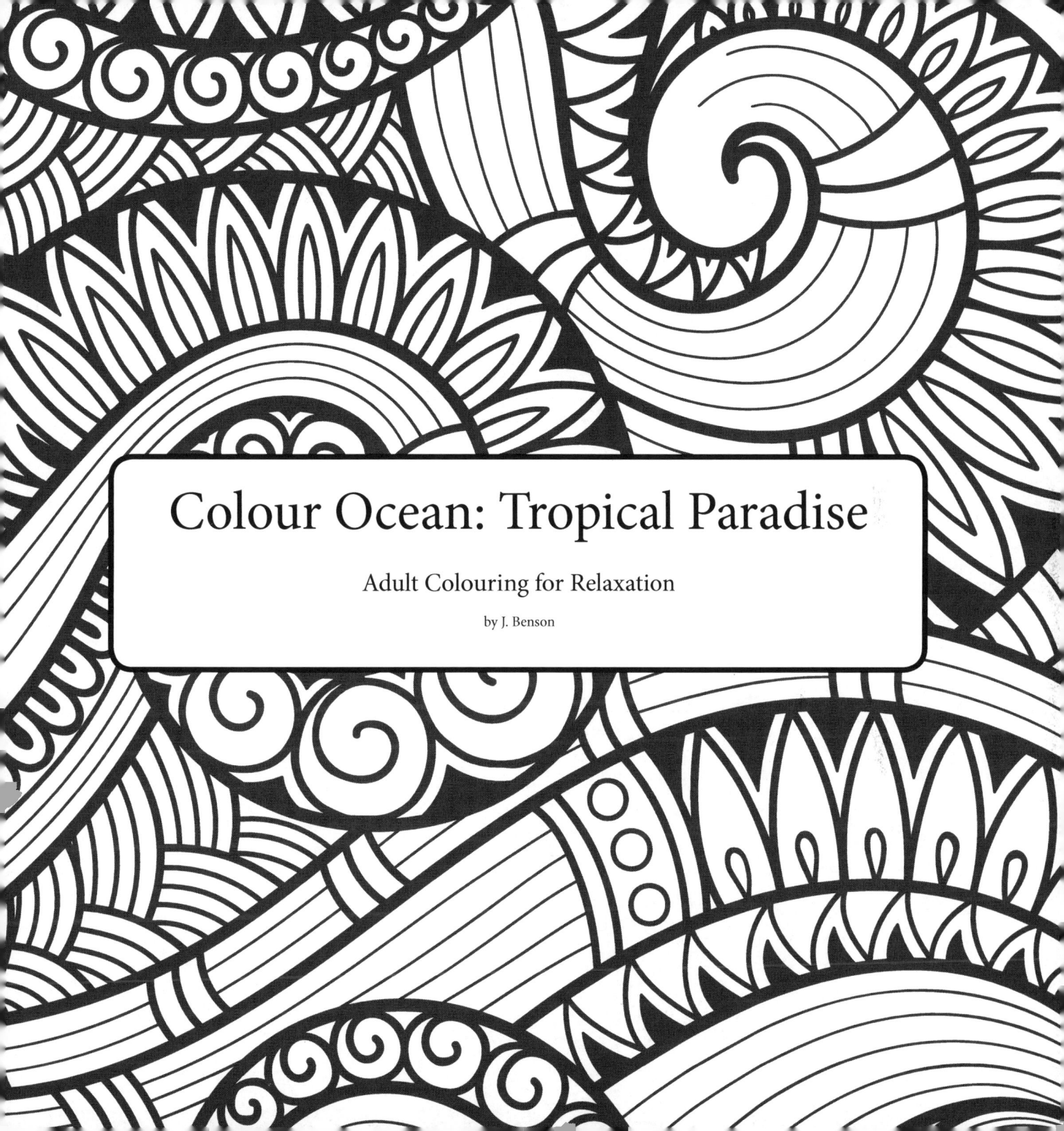

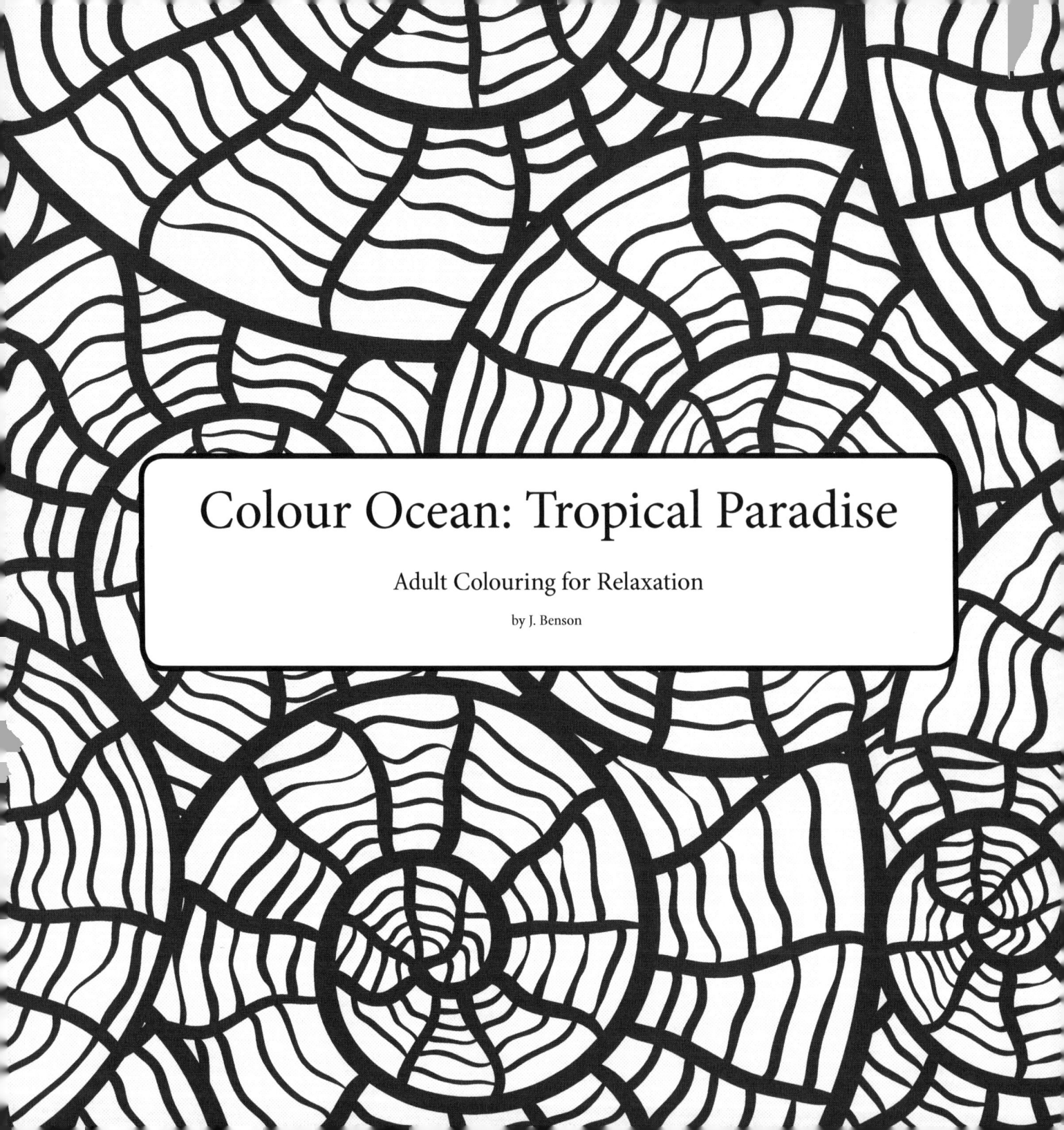

Colour Ocean: Tropical Paradise

Adult Colouring for Relaxation

by J. Benson

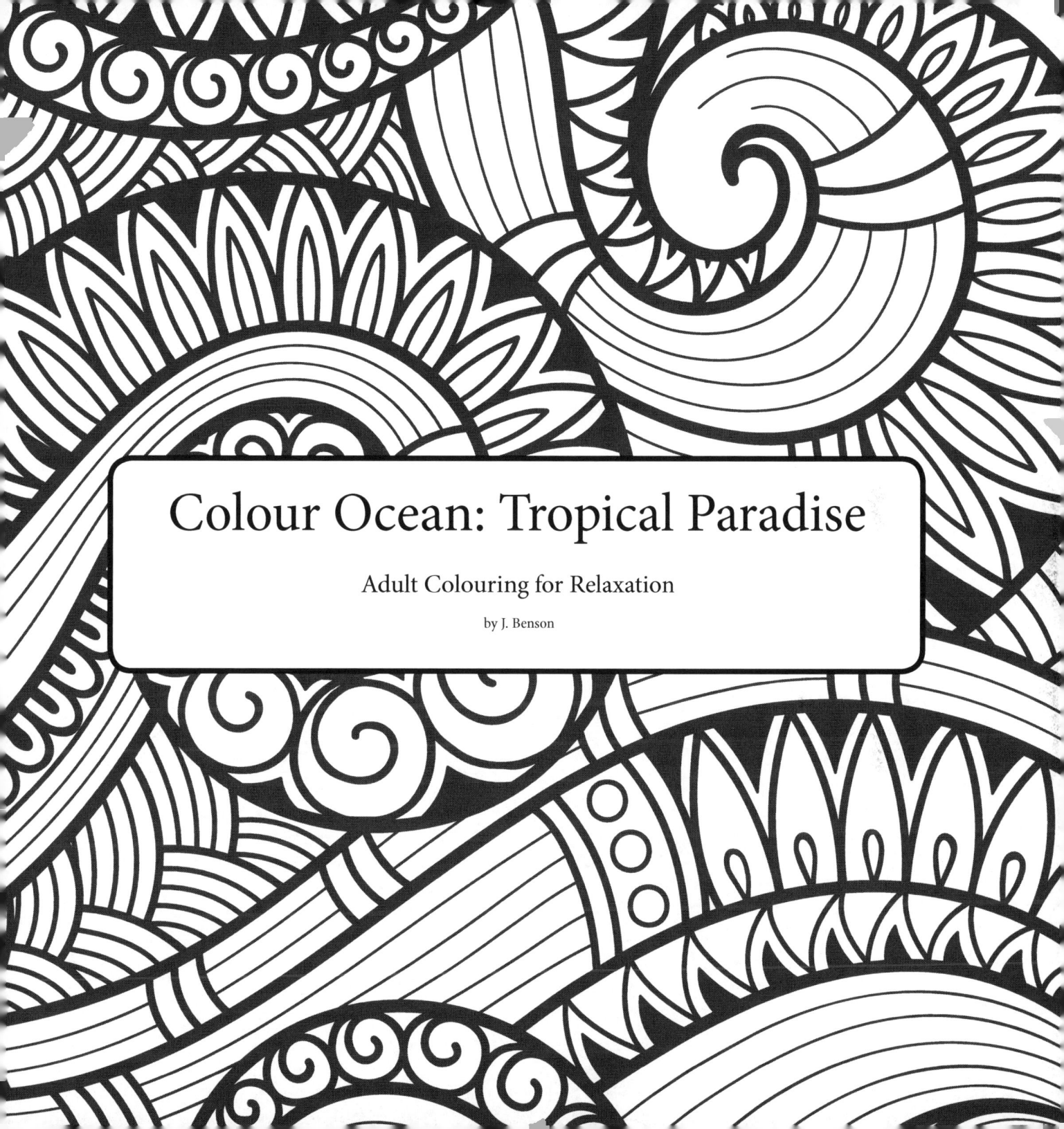

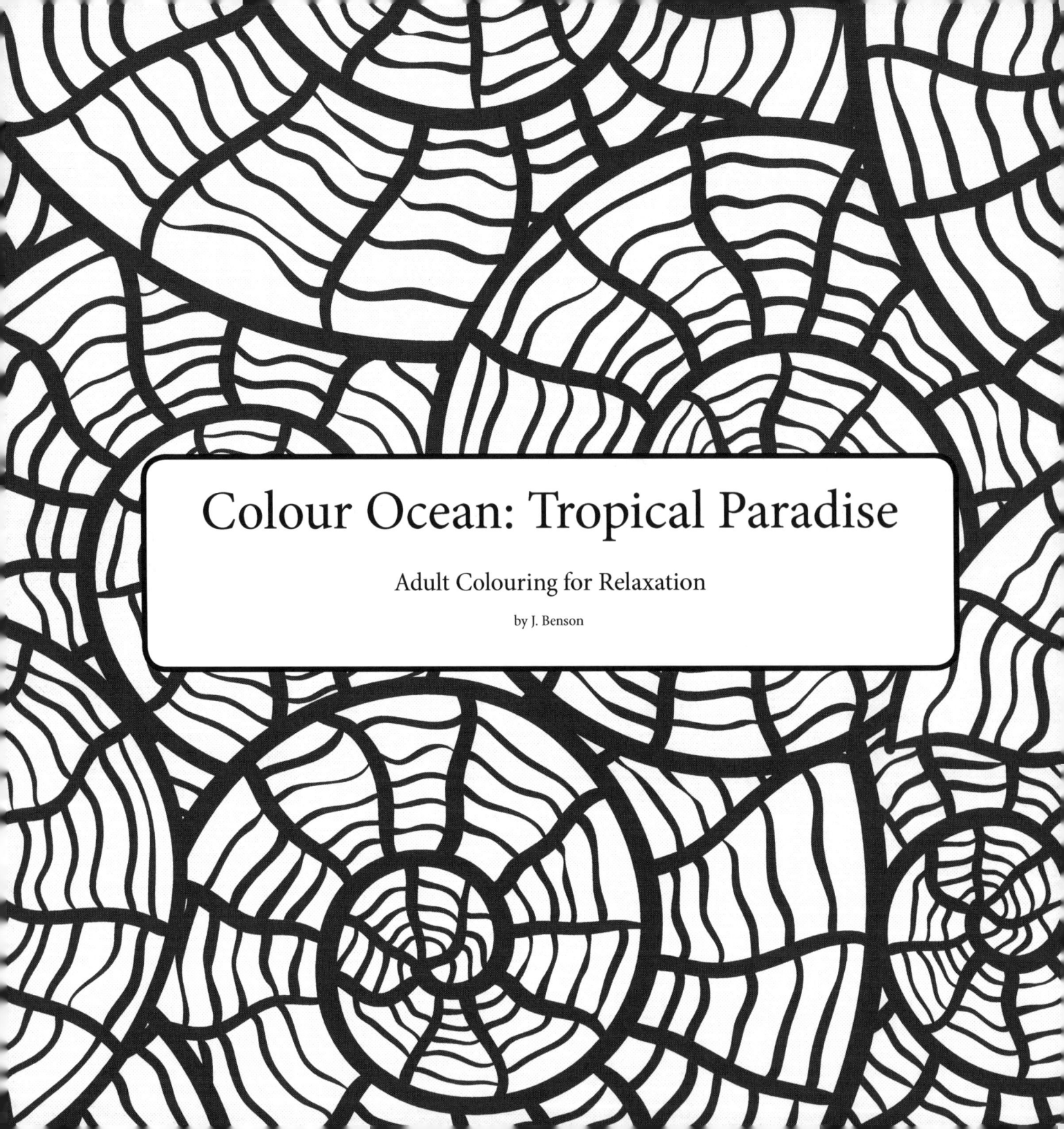

Colour Ocean: Tropical Paradise

Adult Colouring for Relaxation

by J. Benson

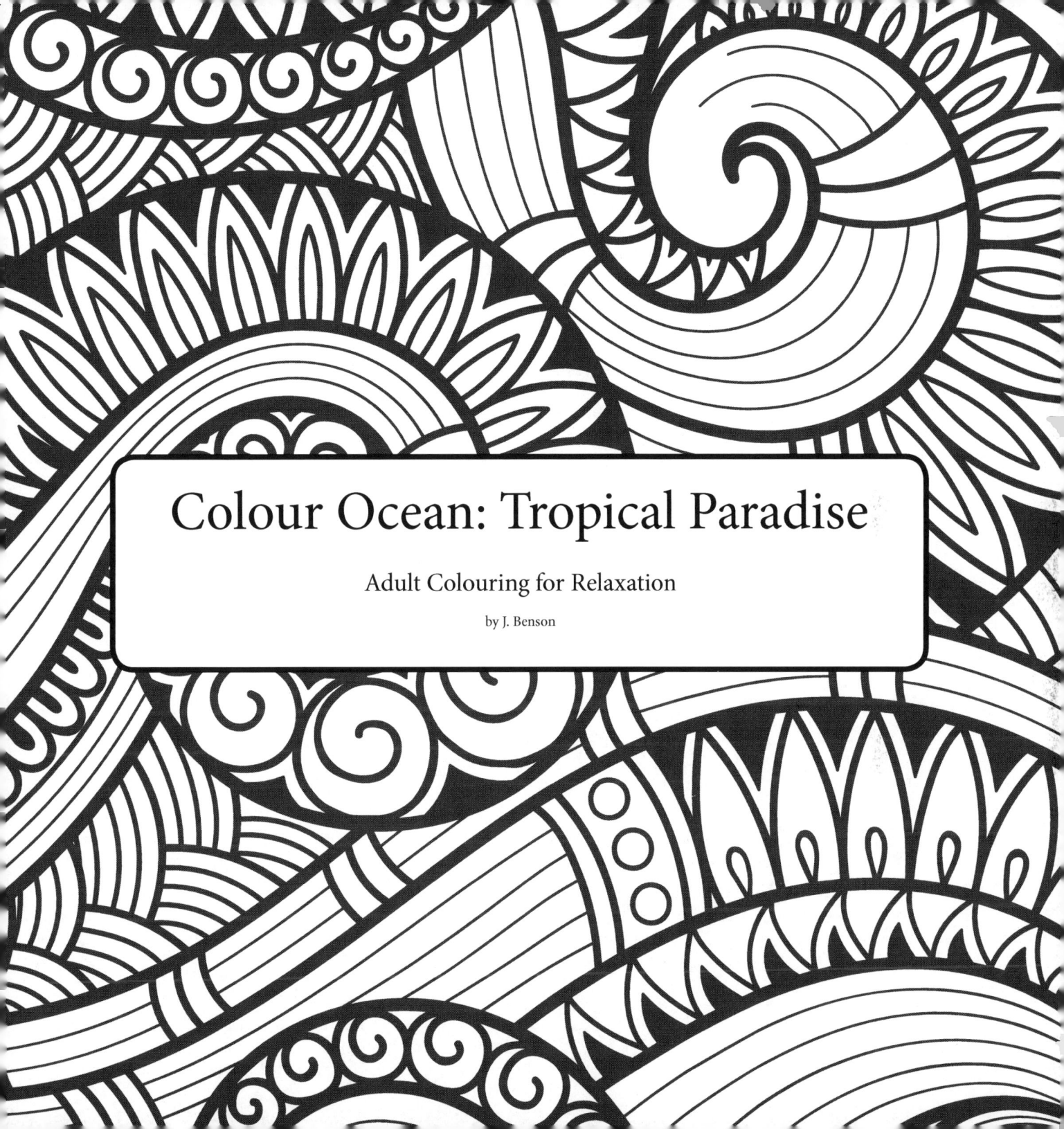

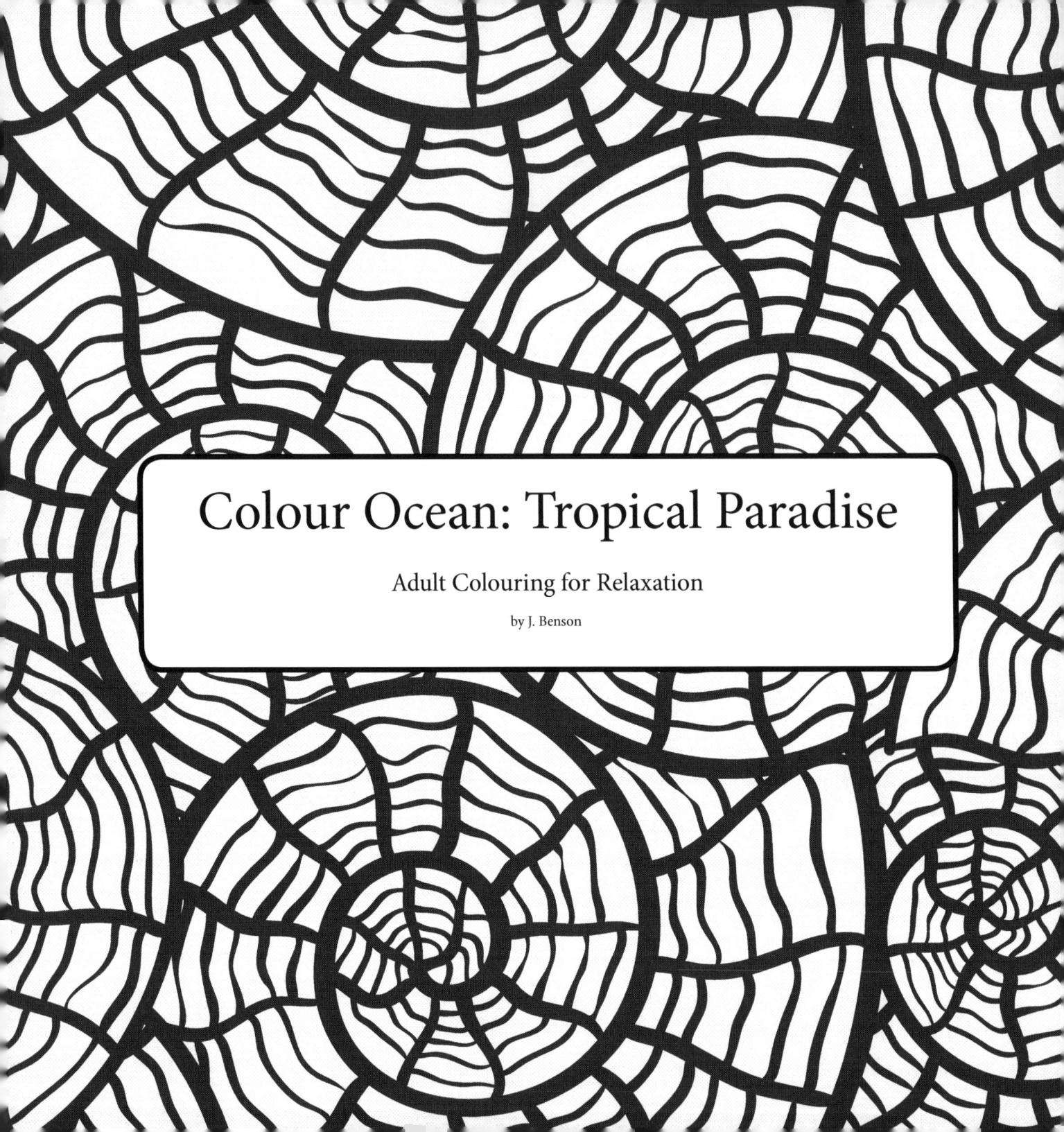

Colour Ocean: Tropical Paradise

Adult Colouring for Relaxation

by J. Benson

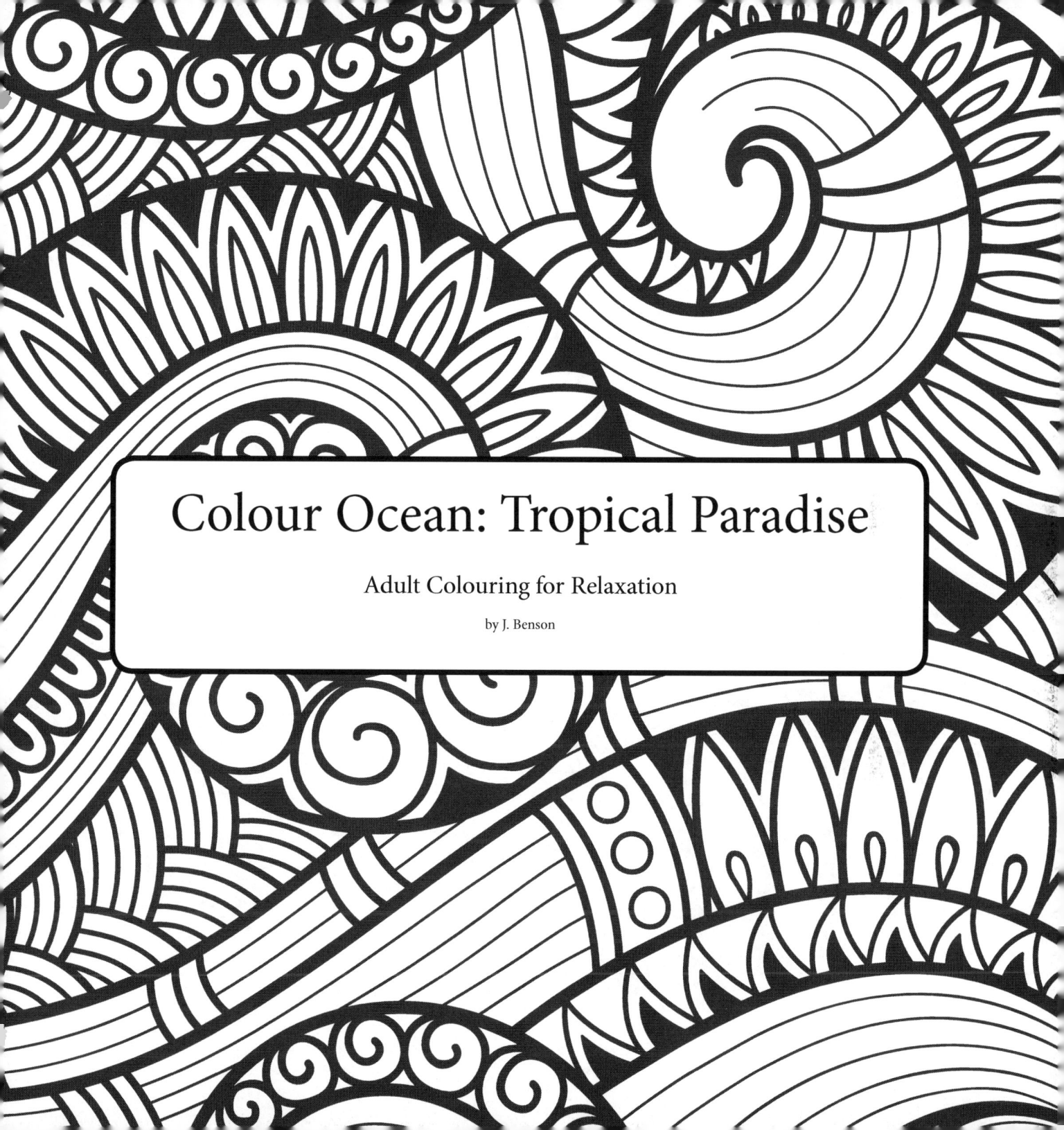

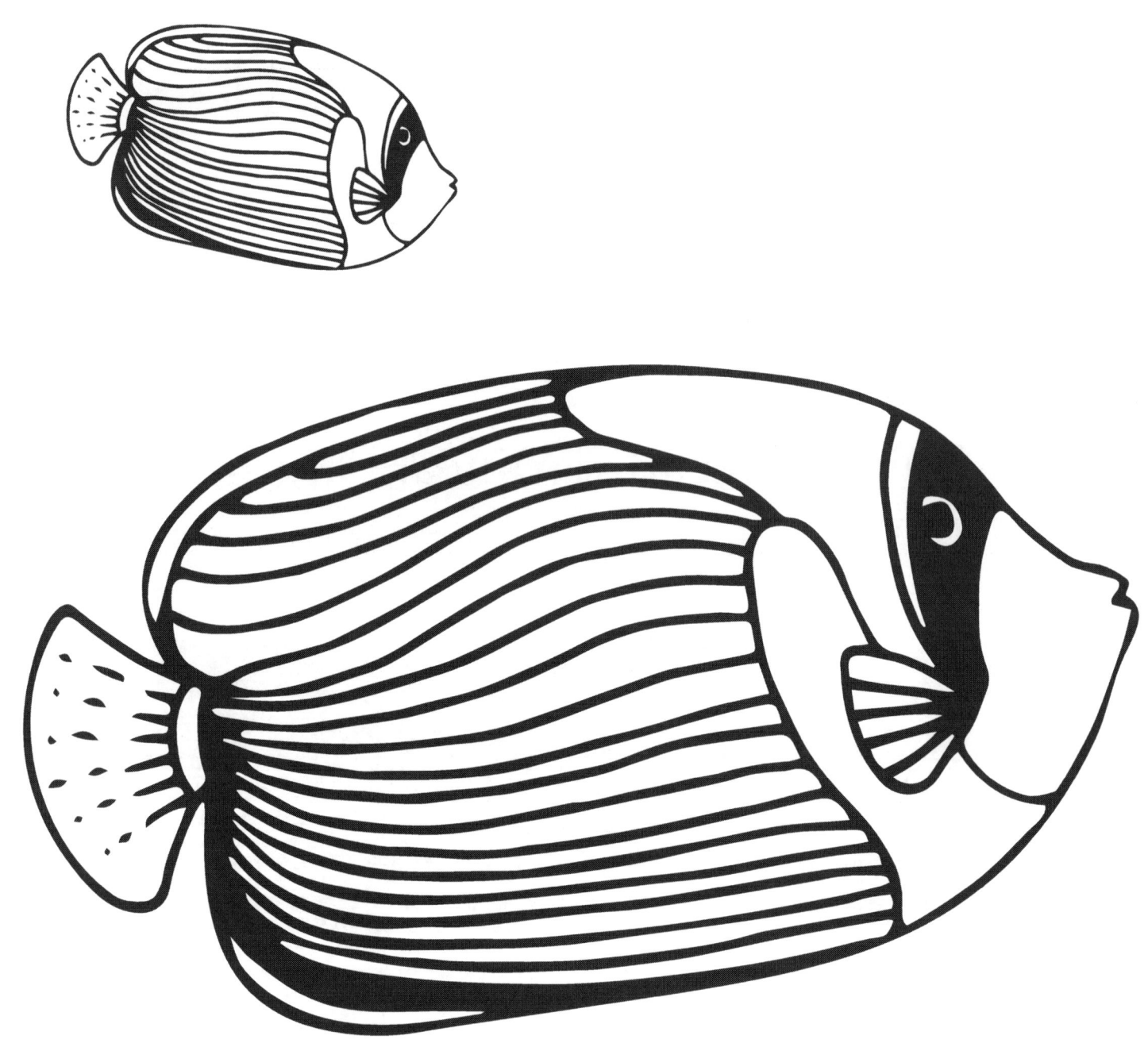

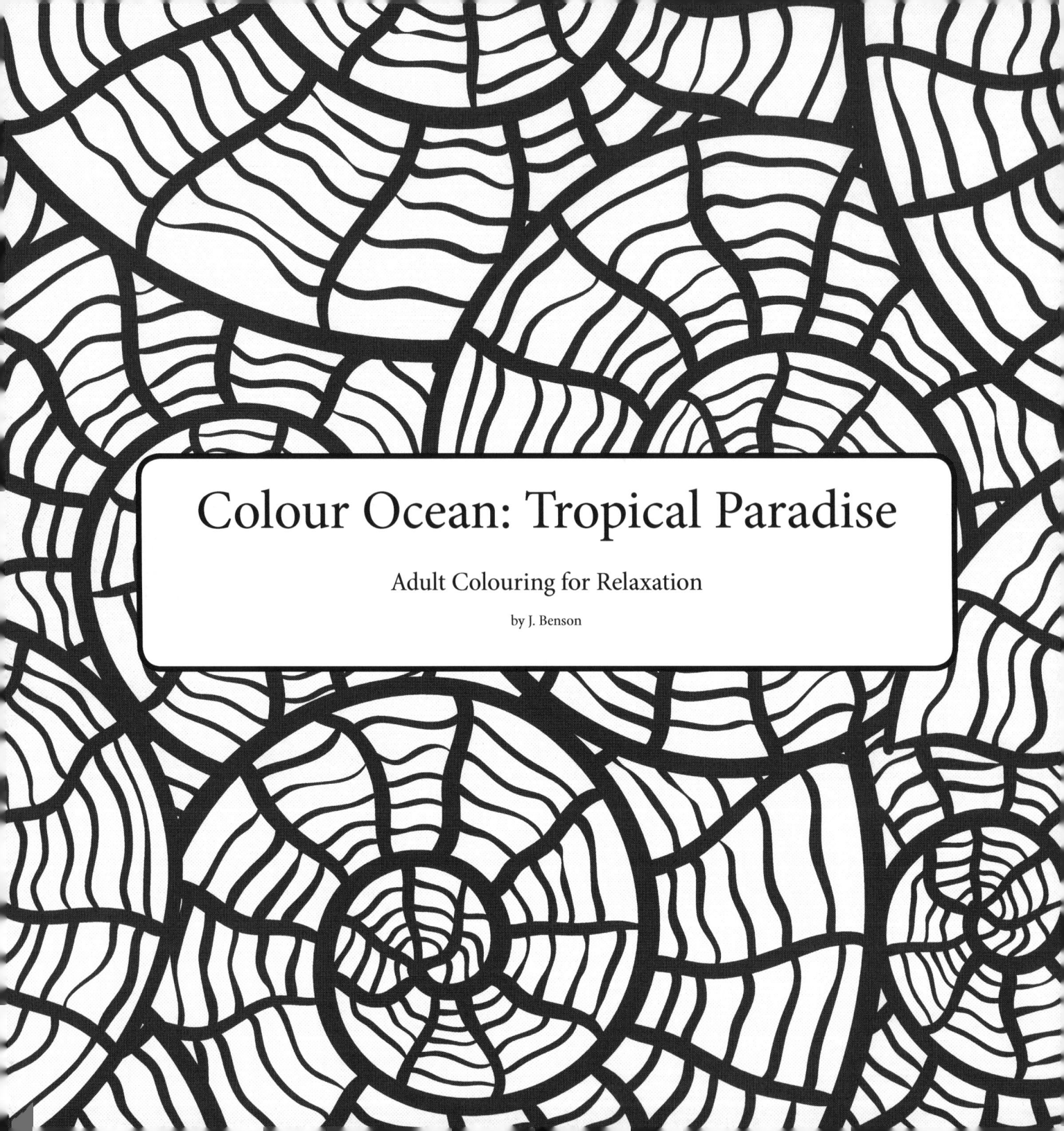

Colour Ocean: Tropical Paradise

Adult Colouring for Relaxation

by J. Benson

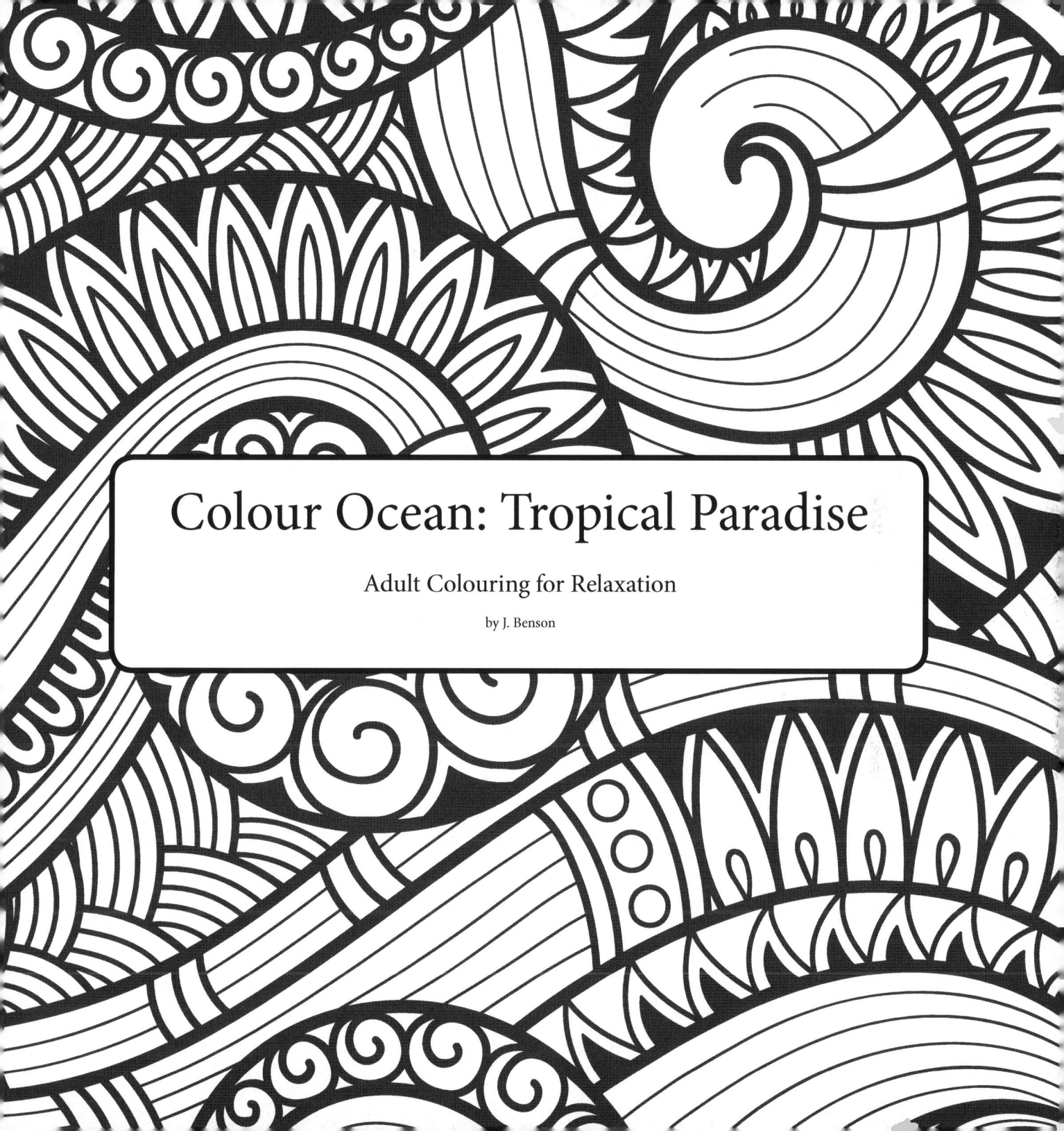

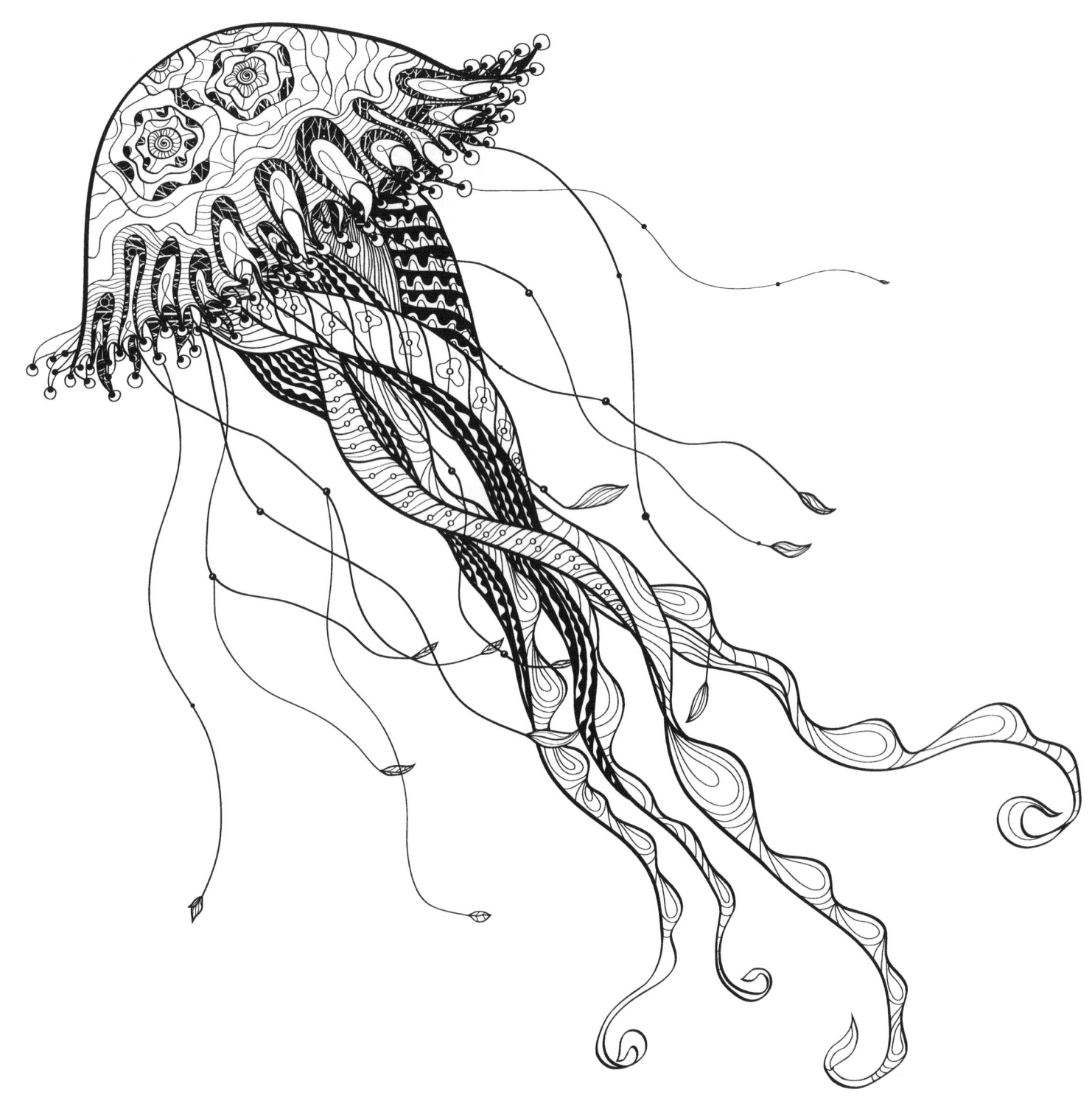

Now that you've completed this book, why not cut out your favourite patterns and share them with the people you care about...

Other books that may be of interest:

Colour Me Zen: Tranquility
Adult Colouring for Relaxation
by J. Benson

Colour Me Zen: Celtic Designs
Adult Colouring for Relaxation
by J. Benson

Colour Me Zen: Ancient Egypt
Adult Colouring for Relaxation
by J. Benson

Colour Me Zen: Mayan Mandalas
Adult Colouring for Relaxation
by J. Benson

available on Amazon now!

Made in the USA
Lexington, KY
04 March 2016